# Motivate ★ BULLETIN ★ ★ BOARDS ★

**by Eva Mae Lee**

(Kindergarten through Grade Five)

illustrated by Richard W. Briggs

STANDARD PUBLISHING
Cincinnati, Ohio

3283

Library of Congress Catalog Card Number 82-80997

ISBN: 0-87239-596-0

# CONTENTS

# INTRODUCTION

The Bible teaches that God loves us and blesses us when we love and obey Him. We need to help children realize that they can enjoy God's blessings from their church-related activities.

Most children respond to love, to our positive acceptance of them, and they want to please. Children as well as adults enjoy recognition for a good performance or improvement. We, as teachers, have the opportunity to plant seeds of love in the lives of those children with whom we work.

Someone has said that people come to church to be loved as well as to hear the Bible. Often children may return to our classes because that is the only place they feel cared about and appreciated. This positive atmosphere will motivate children to learn of God's Word and the one way of salvation through Jesus Christ.

Another benefit to consider is that as students get caught up in working toward goals, the teacher spends less time in counseling and has more time to devote to the lesson.

# HOW TO MOTIVATE WITH BULLETIN BOARDS

Your bulletin boards can be used to motivate students in Sunday school, vacation Bible school, or in a Christian day school. They can teach ideas, encourage students to learn, modify their behavior, and make the room attractive.

The ideas in this book can be modified to accommodate a large bulletin board, a large piece of wrapping paper, small pieces of construction paper that have been taped together, a portable flannelboard, fabric taped to any sturdy board, or just use a chalkboard with colored chalk. Use your imagination and make one work for you in almost any location.

Each board has a theme that is based on a Bible story, holiday season, patriotic idea, or some other appropriate motivational goal. Symbols may be teacher-made or constructed by the students. Third graders and older should be delighted to create their own symbols to move on the boards.

Symbols will move horizontally, vertically, remain stationary, or have additions, depending upon the idea you select. These moves or additions are activated each time the student has prepared a lesson, memorized a Bible verse or chapter, learned the books of the Bible or names of the twelve apostles, been kind to others, listened to the lesson and answered questions, brought a friend to hear about Jesus, etc.

A reward of some type is given to the winner(s) at the end of a specified time. This could be for the week of vacation Bible school; for a month to six weeks or a holiday season; or in Christian schools for a quarter or grading period. It will be easier to decide on the time period after you have selected your idea.

Rewards may range from an attractive plaque (teacher-made) with names of winners, a colorful ribbon, a certificate, or a small gift: a felt marker, cute eraser, or any of the inexpensive items found in your Christian bookstore. Another idea is to keep a record of the winners and number of points so there can be a winner for the year.

With these motivational ideas, you are reinforcing good work habits, encouraging good listening habits, helping students change their daily behavior, and leading them to think for themselves. In the process they learn about the Lord and enjoy doing so. You are patting them on the back and they love it! We all do.

Many students work so hard at achieving that their entire performance changes. They are happy to do their best and you are molding lives by helping your students to enjoy learning about God.

You may not wish to use these reward ideas in your vacation Bible school or Sunday-school classes, but they can be very effective in the classrooms of the Christian day schools.

A demerit can be given or moves lost when interruptions become a problem or lessons aren't prepared. These can be done in a positive way and help the student to see that improvement brings good. These disciplinary measures will be a great help in saving time which might otherwise be required for counseling.

# HORN OF PLENTY

**Motivational objective:** Awareness of God's gifts

Fill the Horn of Plenty with Thanks

**Materials needed:** patterns for letters, scissors, pencil, large sheet of brown paper (may use wrapping paper), construction paper in red, yellow, green, pink, orange, tan, and purple, felt markers, glue, stapler, masking tape

**Directions:**
1. Cut a large cornucopia from the brown paper and add a few swirling lines to give it a bit of depth.
2. Prepare the background and letters.
3. Cut several pieces of fruit for each member.

**Evaluation procedure:**
During class, have the children make a list of all the things that only God can give. Have each member try to name something. As each names one thing, give him or her a piece of fruit to add to the horn. Write the children's names on the fruit or allow each to write their own.

**Optional use:**
After the lesson is over, those who have participated in the singing and actions, brought their Bible, shown a kindness, etc., could add a piece of fruit with his or her name on it.

7

# HELP FIND THE LOST SHEEP

**Motivational objective:** Building the class

**Materials needed:** brown, grey, and black felt markers, shades of brown, tan, and green construction paper, crayons, scissors, a pattern for the shepherd, a measuring stick

## Directions:

1. Cover the board and sketch in mountains or cut them from green and brown paper. Make title letters from dark construction paper.
2. Use yardstick to mark off lines, vertically. Then number between the lines from one to eight, five to forty, or whatever pattern you choose.
3. Cut a shepherd from tan paper for each student. Older children will enjoy designing their own shepherds, but you will need to sketch in the details for younger ones.

## Evaluation procedure:

At the end of the class time, moves could be made for bringing a visitor, two moves for the second time one brings a guest, five moves for the visitor who becomes a member, and one move for reporting on telling others about Jesus.

# FLY YOUR KITE

**Motivational objective:** Class attendance and participation

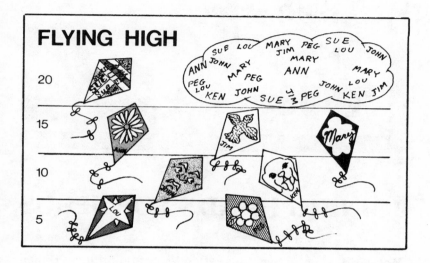

FLYING HIGH

20

15

10

5

**Materials needed:** light blue background material: fabric, paper, or chalk, different colors of construction paper, colored string, felt markers, patterns for lettering, thumbtacks, stapler or masking tape, pencil, measuring stick

**Directions:**
1. Prepare the background and draw horizontal lines. Number the lines from bottom to top by fives.
2. Cut kites from different colored construction paper.
3. Make a white cloud for writing names.

**Evaluation procedure:**
As each student arrives, he or she may move his/her kite up from one number to the next. At the end of the lesson, allow moves for knowing the verse, having Bible, being first to tell what the lesson is about, singing, working well in a group, being cooperative, etc. As each reaches the top, write his/her name on the cloud and he or she begins over again.

**Optional:**
Use a jet plane or rocket instead of a kite.

# JOINING HANDS FOR JESUS

**Motivational objective:** Class attendance and bringing Bibles

**Materials needed:** letter patterns, red, yellow, black, and white construction paper, scissors, pencil, masking tape, stapler, felt marker or broad pointed pen and ink, pattern for children

**Directions:**
1. Cut lots of boys and girls from the four colors of construction paper.
2. Prepare the background or just designate a place on the wall.
3. Use masking tape, torn into about 1 inch pieces and rolled, for attaching the boys and girls to the wall. These rolls of tape may also be used for putting up the lettering.

**Evaluation procedure:**
When the lesson is over, each child in attendance may have his or her name put on one of the boys or girls and placed in a circle. They may also add to the circle for bringing their Bibles to class or bringing a visitor. You may use this idea for a quarter or whatever designated time you wish. Children love watching the circle grow.

# BALANCE YOUR WORLD

**Motivational objective:** Class participation

**Materials needed:**
  A. white background material, blue and gray construction paper, blue paint or felt markers, small black felt marker, scissors, glue, stapler
  B. globe of the world and white paper

**Directions:**
  1. Cut a gray seal and a blue sphere for the nose of each.
  2. Sketch in map of the world on each sphere, if you wish.
  3. You may draw blue ripples on the white background with paint or felt marker to represent water.
  4. Then place the seals in the water.

**Evaluation procedure:**
  A. When the lesson is over, those members who have: brought a visitor, learned the Bible verse, shown a kindness in class, followed directions, plan to stay for church, bowed head during prayer, etc., may have their name written on their world.
  B. All or any of the above may have their names written on a strip of white paper and stuck on the globe. The winner would be the one who had his or her name written the greatest number of times.

# BE A WISE-MAN

**Motivational objective:** Class participation

**Materials needed:** patterns for letters and camel and wise-man, light beige or white, dark blue, and yellow construction paper, felt markers, scissors, stapler, crayons, measuring stick, thumbtacks, Scotch or masking tape

**Directions:**
1. Prepare the background and draw six vertical and evenly spaced lines. Number these by ones or fives.
2. Cut a large star from the yellow paper or just use a commercial nativity scene. Place on the side where you have the highest number on your vertical lines.
3. Cut letters and attach to top of board with tiny rolls of masking tape or staple them.
4. Make a wise-man on his camel for each participant.

**Evaluation procedure:**
When the lesson is over, each child who has participated in the class, brought his or her Bible, reported on a good deed, brought a friend, joined in the singing, or brought an offering, may move his or her wise-man toward the star or nativity scene. Keep a record of points for each child so you can reward them at the end of your designated time.

12

# DECORATE THE TREE

**Motivational objective:** Class participation or Bible learning

**Materials needed:** Large sheet of green construction paper, lots of different colors and shades in smaller pieces of paper, felt markers, scissors, glue, stapler

### Directions:
1. Fold the green paper in half and cut both sides of the tree at once, then staple it to the board or glue to the background. You may substitute a white paper tree on a blue background for a very effective board.
2. Supply small pieces of many colors of paper. You will need lots of white, blue, green, and red.
3. Allow students to select a symbol to make: a candy cane, star, ornament, nativity scene, snowman, angel, stocking, gift, etc. Each can make several of one kind.

### Evaluation procedure:
After the lesson, each child who has been a good listener, sat quietly during prayer, known the Bible verse, learned the song, brought a Bible, etc., could add one of his or her ornaments to the tree. At the end of the month or the designated period of time, the one with the most ornaments wins a prize.

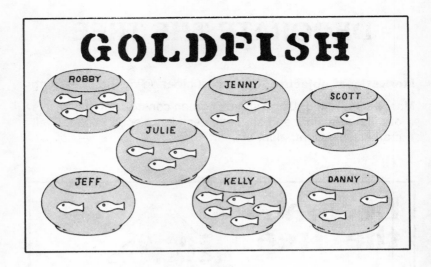

# GOLDFISH

**Motivational objective:** Class participation

**Materials needed:** background material, large sheet of light blue or white construction paper, letter patterns, pencil, scissors, tape, stapler, felt markers

**Directions:**
1. Prepare the background on a board, chalkboard, or box.
2. Sketch individual bowls and attach, or use one large bowl if you prefer.
3. Cut goldfish from yellow, orange, or gold paper. You will need many of these. They may be various sizes and shapes. However, your class may enjoy making their own if time permits.
4. If you use one large fishbowl, the children's names may be written on their fish when added.

**Evaluation procedure:**
Each person who has participated in the lesson by singing, answering questions about the lesson, saying the Bible verse, or whatever is appropriate, may add a fish to his or her individual bowl or to the large bowl.

# THE GOOD APPLE TREE

**Motivational objective:** Class participation

**Materials needed:** dark brown, red, green, and yellow construction paper, felt-tipped marker or crayon, light-colored paper for background

The Good Apple Tree

**Directions:**
1. Cover the board and make letters for the title.
2. Sketch a large tree on the light shade of paper or background material using a felt-tipped marker or crayon.
3. You may cut the tree from brown construction paper if you wish.
4. Cut lots of red and yellow apples and green leaves from construction paper and place them on the tree.

**Evaluation procedure:**
At the end of the Sunday-school lesson, each student who has contributed to the lesson, joined in the singing, been kind to others in class, etc., may have his or her name written on an apple.

**Optional:**
Cut a basket from brown paper for each child's apples.

When a child gets his or her name on five apples, you may wish to remove them from the tree and arrange them in the child's basket. Or, you may have an extra basket and several very large apples on which to write the names of the children who get their names on as many as five or more apples on the tree.

# Help Jonathan Practice Shooting

**SCOREBOARD**

| | |
|---|---|
| Chris | III |
| Tom | THL |
| Mary | IIII |
| Connie | THL I |
| Ken | III |
| Mark | THL I |
| Tammy | III |
| Gary | IIII |

# HELP JONATHAN PRACTICE

**Motivational objective:** Class participation

**Materials needed:**
- A. chalkboard and chalk, arrows from any colored paper, talley sheet, scissors, marker
- B. background material, large sheet of butcher paper, construction paper, or poster board, felt markers, letter patterns, light-colored paper for arrows or darts, thumbtacks

**Directions:**
1. Prepare the background or chalkboard and make the bull's-eye.
2. Cut a dart or an arrow for each member and write their names on them.
3. Cut out the letters or print them on the chalkboard.
4. Keep a scoreboard for the points.

**Evaluation procedure:**
At the end of your time with the class, each child who has completed a project, known the Bible verse, sat quietly during the lesson and prayer, brought a visitor, joined in the singing, etc., may move his or her arrow toward the center. Allow one move per activity or acceptable answer. As each reaches the bull's-eye, write his or her name in the center or on a separate sheet of paper on the board.

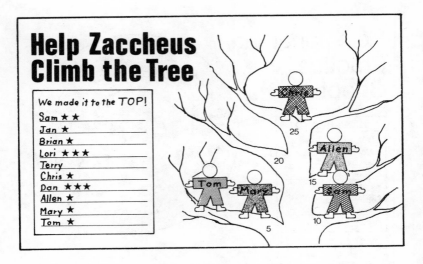

**Help Zaccheus Climb the Tree**

We made it to the TOP!

Sam ★ ★
Jan ★
Brian ★
Lori ★ ★ ★
Terry
Chris ★
Dan ★ ★ ★
Allen ★
Mary ★
Tom ★

# HELP ZACCHEUS CLIMB

**Motivational objective:** Class participation

**Materials needed:** light blue for background, green, tan, and white construction paper, felt markers, scissors, crayons, glue or stapler, thumbtacks

**Directions:**
1. Sketch a tall tree on the background with a pencil and then go over the sketch with a felt marker or dark crayon.
2. Number the branches from the bottom up.
3. Add a few green leaves cut from construction paper if you wish.
4. Cut a symbol for Zaccheus from tan or white construction paper. You may color or allow children to do so.

**Evaluation procedure:**
When class is over, each child may move his or her "Zaccheus" from one number to the next, vertically, for each activity in which he or she has participated. These could include: learning the Bible verse, listening and answering in class, sharing craft items with others, doing the actions to the songs, bringing a visitor, etc. Each time a member gets to the top branch, his or her name could be written there or on a separate slip of paper attached to the board. Give a prize at the end of the designated time for the most points.

# HIDE MOSES' ARK

**Motivational objective:** Class participation

**Materials needed:** light background material, dark paper for letters, patterns for letters, brown construction paper, green felt marker or green paper, blue paint or paper, stapler, thumbtacks

## Directions:

1. Prepare the background and measure vertical lines about six to ten inches apart. (Smaller boards may need smaller spaces.) Number the spaces.
2. Cut bulrushes from green paper and glue or staple to the background.
3. Cut little arks from brown construction paper for each member and let each write his or her name on an ark.
4. Make water from blue paper, paints, or crayons.

## Evaluation procedure:

At the end of the period, students who know the lesson, have participated in the singing and actions, brought a Bible, or shown a kindness could move their arks one space across the board. Keep a sheet of paper on the board to enter the names of those who have completed the cycle. Then each begins again.

# HIT A HOME RUN FOR JESUS

**Motivational objective:** Class participation or good deeds

**Materials needed:** green paper for background and black felt marker, or white background with a green marker, assorted colors of construction paper, thumbtacks, scissors, crayons

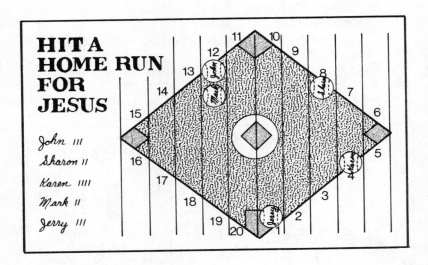

## Directions:
1. Cover the board with green or white paper.
2. Sketch baseball field with bases and mounds.
3. Mark off vertical lines with black marker and number them.
4. Allow students to make a symbol such as a bat, baseball, cap, player, etc. (Teacher may make these for the little people.)

## Evaluation procedure:
At the end of the lesson or class, members could move around the field from one line to another for: being on time, being kind to an older person and reporting it to the class, listening attentively, staying in line, etc.

# HOSANNA TO THE SON OF DAVID

**Motivational objective:** Class participation

**Materials needed:** green paper: either construction or tissue, scissors, glue or stapler, large blue, white, or tan covering for the bulletin board, picture of Jesus on a donkey, an opaque projector if available

**Directions:**
1. Cover your board, sketch a road as shown, and make the letters for the title.
2. Use any means such as an opaque projector to copy and enlarge the picture of Jesus on the donkey. (Optional: Use an appropriate picture of Jesus from a flannelgraph packet or a Bible-story paper.)
3. Sketch in the city of Jerusalem on the left side.
4. Cut many palm branches from the green paper.

**Evaluation procedure:**
At the end of the Sunday-school lesson, give palm branches to each one who has listened attentively, sat still during story time, joined in the singing, bowed head in prayer, etc. Names may be printed on the palm branches if you use them for more than one Sunday. (Suggestion: this board is very effective for several Sundays before Easter.)

# THE JEWEL BOX

**Motivational objective:** Class participation

**Materials needed:** a felt marker, colored construction paper, thumbtacks, tape or stapler, material for background, shiny wrapping paper if available

**Directions:**
1. Cover the board and make the letters.
2. Sketch a chest or box on your background, then go over it with the felt marker.
3. Have a box of colored paper for students to use in making their jewels, or have teacher-made jewels ready for use.

**Evaluation procedure:**
At the end of the lesson, each child could add a jewel to the box if he or she has contributed to the lesson, sat quietly on a chair or in a group, brought a Bible to class, used a soft voice, or been a good listener.

**Optional:**
The chest can be cut from lucite or heavy plastic. It will show up better if you go around the edges with black.

# MAKE RAYS OF SUNSHINE

**Motivational objective:** Class participation

**Materials needed:** large sheet of bright yellow construction paper, several sheets of red, yellow, and orange (or shades of these), material for a light background, glue, thumbtacks, felt markers or paints

**Directions:**
1. Cover the board with a light background and make dark letters for the title.
2. Cut a large round sun from the large sheet of yellow construction paper and make a happy face on it. Place it in the center of the board or on a wall.
3. Cut long, thin triangles for "rays" from the reds, yellows, and oranges.

**Evaluation procedure:**
After the Sunday-school lesson, each child could put up a ray for bringing a new member, lesson participation, showing good citizenship, answering questions about the story, or helping clean up after the craft activity. Be sure to write each student's name on all his or her rays.

# REACH A STAR

**Motivational objective:** Class participation

**Materials needed:** large sheet of yellow construction paper, (or orange felt marker, yellow yarn), black felt marker, background material, letters, more yellow or orange paper for small stars, glue or stapler, scissors

**Directions:**
1. Prepare the background and cut letters for caption.
2. Make a large star from yellow construction paper or staple the yarn into the shape of a star. Another idea is to sketch an orange or yellow star on a white background. Place your star on the right side of the background.
3. Sketch in the stairs or steps with black felt marker and number them.
4. Make a star for each child.

**Evaluation procedure:**
When the lesson is finished, each member who has been a good listener, brought his or her Bible to class, brought a visitor, reported on a good deed, read the lesson, or participated in some way may move his or her star up a step toward the large star. Write the children's names on the large star as each reaches it. At the end of the month or unit, reward those whose names are written the most on the large star.

# SPIRITUAL VITAMINS

**Motivational objective:** Class participation

**Materials needed:** scissors, glue, tape, felt markers, several colors of construction paper for students, one whole sheet of construction paper for each member's bottle, patterns for bottles and vitamins, background materials

**Directions:**
1. Cover the board with a light background and cut letters from dark paper that will show up well with the bottles.
2. Sketch large bottles, one for each child and write his or her name on the lid. These may be cut from bright-colored paper such as purple, green, orange, or blue.
3. For the younger children, cut lots of vitamins to put in their bottles. Older students will want to make their own. Some will want all one color while others may want a variety.

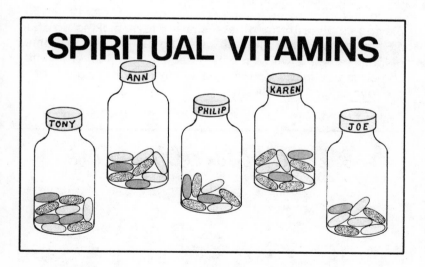

**Evaluation procedure:**

When the lesson is over, students who have lined up quietly, told the main idea of the lesson, learned the Bible verse, learned how to spell J E S U S, or whatever your goals were, may put a vitamin in his or her jar for each.

# LET THE SON SHINE OUT

**Motivational objective:** Doing good deeds

**Materials needed:** yellow and orange construction paper, gold foil paper, paints or felt markers, dark paper for letters, light shade of paper or fabric for a background, tape, glue or stapler

**Directions:**
1. Cover your board with the light paper or fabric.
2. Cut letters from orange or bright gold paper for the title.
3. Use yellow construction paper and cut lots and lots of suns and happy faces.
4. Cover the board with happy faces and use the suns later as covers.

**Evaluation procedure:**
After the lesson, give the students a sun for each good deed completed. Print the good deed on the sun with the child's name. Then cover a happy face with the good deed. The suns could be for: showing a good attitude during the craft period, playing kindly with the others, sharing toys, picking up after an activity, sharing with the class about helping at home, helping someone with a project, reading the Bible, or inviting someone to church. You could use any idea that would show the love of God for others.

Bring Noah's Animals into the Ark

# NOAH'S ANIMALS

**Motivational objective:** Doing good deeds

**Materials needed:** large sheet(s) of gray or brown paper, smaller pieces of beige, white, or light-colored construction paper, crayons, scissors, glue, letter patterns, felt markers, masking tape, ditto masters, an opaque projector

### Directions:
1. Prepare the background, complete with letters.
2. Cut an ark from brown or gray paper, or sketch it with a pencil and go over the sketch with a dark felt marker.
3. Make a ditto of several different animals for each student. Optional idea would be to allow the children to make their own animals.
4. Names should be written on each child's animals as they are placed in the ark.
5. If each child chooses only one particular animal, you may use a key in the corner of the board with each child's name and the animal he or she has chosen.

### Evaluation procedure:
At the end of the Sunday-school lesson, each child who has shared the craft items, reported on a good deed, told how he or she has been helpful at home, helped put games away, lined up quietly for drinks or snacks, or been courteous, could put animals in the ark.

# STARS IN MY CROWN

**Motivational objective:** Doing good deeds

**Materials needed:** yellow, gold, or purple construction paper, stars (commercial or teacher-made), background material

**Directions:**
1. Use dark blue construction paper for the background or any other color or material you wish. Just be sure it is attractive so the children will enjoy seeing their crowns displayed. Cut letters for the title from a lighter color for contrast.
2. Cut crowns from construction paper for each child, or let them design and cut their own.
3. Write each child's name on his or her crown.

**Evaluation procedure:**
Attach stars to the crowns as the children report on the good deeds they have done during the week.

# TOOLS FOR GOOD DEEDS

**Motivational objective:** Doing good deeds

**Materials needed:** large sheet of brown wrapping paper or poster board or inexpensive fabric for background, different colors of construction paper for making tools

**Directions:**
1. Cover the board and make the letters for the title.
2. You may wish to make rows of dots to look like peg board for hanging tools.
3. Cut many different shapes of tools for your children to hang on the peg board. Older children may want to make their own.
4. Make patterns for the tools from heavy paper if the children need guides.

**Evaluation procedure:**
When the class is over, students may put up different tools for being kind to others, sharing materials during the craft activity, reporting on their good deeds for the week, keeping quiet in line, or sitting quietly during story time. Let the children choose the particular tool they like best.

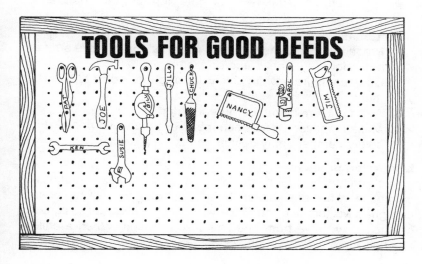

# TRAVEL TO GOD'S FARTHEST PLANET

**Motivational objective:** Doing good deeds and class participation

**Materials needed:** background material of blue paper or fabric (optional would be chalkboard and colored chalk), white paper, box of crayons, scissors, thumbtacks, tape, letter patterns, stapler, Plasti-Tak or glue, felt markers, paints

**Directions:**
1. Prepare background with blue paper or chalk, make orbital paths for the planets, and add lettering.
2. Cut planets from white construction paper, color, and label them.
3. Arrange planets in their proper order.
4. Make a spaceship for each member from white paper and color. Members may design and color their own.

**Evaluation procedure:**
Each child who has made a call to an absentee, brought a member who has been absent for a time, brought a new member, brought a visitor, said the Bible verse, or learned an assigned chapter, may move from one planet to the next. When a child reaches Pluto, write that child's name on Pluto.

# HANDS THAT HELP JESUS

**Motivational objective:** Encouraging good deeds and being helpful

**Materials needed:** orange background, yellow construction paper, stapler, pencil, black felt marker, letter patterns, scissors, thumbtacks

## Directions:
1. Prepare the background.
2. Cut letters and darken the edges with a black marker.
3. Allow class members to draw around their hands on the yellow construction paper with a pencil. Then they should darken the outlines with a black felt marker.
4. Let the children write their own names on the hands.
5. Optional colors could be shades of green or blue or mix those two colors.

## Evaluation procedure:
When the lesson is over, those who have reported on good deeds done at home, been helpful in class, followed directions in class, helped a neighbor, lined up quietly, sat still so others could hear the lesson, bowed head during prayer, etc., may have a star or check for each on his or her hand.

## Optional:
Use many small hands for a small class.

# HELP JOASH REPAIR THE TEMPLE OF GOD

**Motivational objective:** Encouraging giving

**Materials needed:** large sheet of brown paper, yellow or gold construction paper, scissors, pencil, stapler, glue, masking tape, felt markers, patterns for letters

**Directions:**
1. Prepare background and lettering.
2. Sketch a large chest on the background or cut it from the brown paper.
3. Cut many coins from the yellow or gold paper.

**Evaluation procedure:**
When the class is over, those who have brought an offering for the class, for the building fund, for the needy, or for missionaries, may add a coin with his or her name written on it.

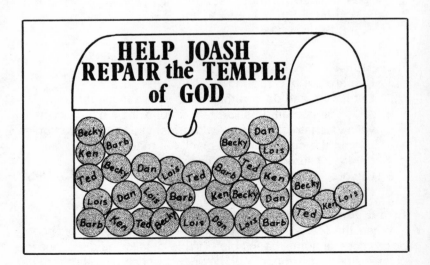

**Optional use:**
Class participation, learning books of the Bible, memorizing a chapter, bringing a new member, etc.

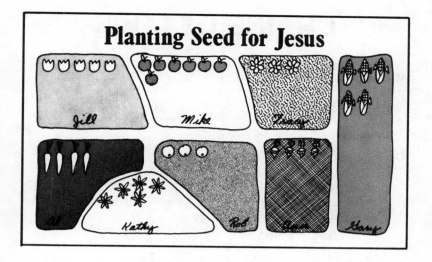

# PLANTING SEED

**Motivational objective:** Encouraging witnessing

**Materials needed:** a large board and light background material, felt markers in black or a dark color, lots of different colored construction paper, glue, Scotch tape, stapler, scissors, a box of crayons or paints

### Directions:
1. Cover the board with the light background material.
2. Block off random "plots" for your garden, one for each child, and write names in the plots. Taller students might have the highest areas.
3. Cut out letters from dark paper for the title or write it in cursive.
4. Prepare a basket or box full of different colors of paper so members may make their own items for their own plot. Let them be imaginative!

### Evaluation procedure:
When the lesson is complete, allow children to make a flower, fruit, or vegetable to plant in their garden. These may be planted for: telling others about Jesus and reporting it to the class, bringing a visitor, having a visitor become a member, or some other deed that would show they have shared the love of God.

# CHAINS OF LOVE

**Motivational objective:** Showing love for God

**Materials needed:** light-colored paper or fabric for the background, felt-tipped marker, glue, tape, stapler, different colors of construction paper

**Directions:**
1. Cover the board with white or any light-colored construction paper. Attach the title letters across the top, and under them, put strips of paper on which you have written the children's names.
2. Cut strips of paper about ½ x 5 inches from construction paper. You may use one color for each child or just have an assortment. Much depends upon the class size.

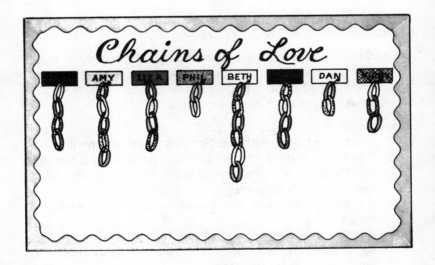

**Evaluation procedure:**
  When class is over, each member who has brought a visitor, completed an activity, brought their Bible to class, been first to find a reference, or shown extra consideration to someone, may add a link to his or her chain. The longest chain maker is the winner.

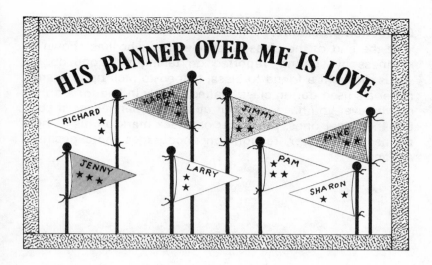

# HIS BANNER OVER ME IS LOVE

**Motivational objective:** Showing the love of God through actions

**Materials needed:** background covering or use a chalkboard, letter patterns, pencils, scissors, crayons, a black felt marker, red, blue, green, yellow, and orange construction paper, stapler, masking tape

**Directions:**
1. Prepare the background in a light shade and cut letters from the construction paper, alternating the colors.
2. Edging the letters in black can be very effective.
3. Cut a banner for each member and write his or her name on it.
4. Draw a staff for each banner with the felt marker.
5. Optional idea is to cut many small banners if you have only a few children. For this activity, you will need one large banner on which to write the names of the children who get five points or a specified number of small banners.

**Evaluation procedure:**

At the end of the class, each member who has shown a kindness by sharing, reported on telling someone about Jesus, brought a friend to class, helped to pick up toys and materials used during class, waited quietly in line for a drink or whatever you have, may put up a small banner, or, if you use the larger ones, put a star or check mark on his or her banner. Remember, recognition encourages more positive actions!

# SKIING HIGH

**Motivational objective:** Showing love for Christ by our actions

**Materials needed:** dark blue or purple background, white paint, cotton, or crayon for snow, pencil, measuring stick, black felt marker, white, tan, and green construction paper, Scotch tape, thumbtacks, scissors, assorted crayons, yarn

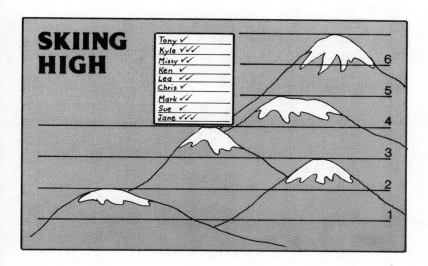

### Directions:
1. Lightly sketch mountains on the background and go over them with a felt marker. Put snow on the mountains with white crayon, cotton, or paint.
2. Optional: Fold strips of green paper and cut pine trees. Attach them across the bottom of the mountains.
3. Draw horizontal lines and number from bottom to top.
4. Cut ski men or other appropriate symbols from light-colored paper and allow children to decorate them. Add Scotch tape to backs of figures for reinforcement.

### Evaluation procedure:
After the story, each child who has participated in class, joined in the singing, helped someone during the handwork, etc., may move up on the board. As each reaches the highest line, write his or her name on the top peak.

# BLOSSOMING FOR CHRIST

**Motivational objective:** Learning the Scriptures

**Materials needed:** material for light background, black felt marker, large sheet of black paper, green tissue paper for leaves, yellow, white, and orange tissue paper (shades of pinks and reds or the purples and lavenders) for blossoms, glue, scissors, letter patterns

**Directions:**
1. Prepare the background. If you use paper, you may wish to sketch a large tree with a felt marker. If you use fabric, you may prefer using black (or brown) paper.
2. Cut leaves of various sizes from the green tissue paper.
3. From the other shades of tissue paper, cut lots and lots of 2 inch squares. These may be kept in separate boxes, according to color.
4. Construction paper may be used in place of tissue, but the tissue gives a 3-D effect.

**Evaluation procedure:**
At the end of the Sunday-school lesson, each child who knows the assigned Bible verse, chapter, part of a chapter, books of the Bible, etc. may add a blossom to the tree. You may use the leaves for attendance, and select a color for each of the assigned memory selections and other activities.

Learned Song
Bowed Head in Prayer
Learned Bible Verse
Attendance

**Blossoming for Christ**

# BUILD A SNOW FORT

**Motivational objective:** Learning about the Bible

**Materials needed:** letter patterns, bright background material, pencils, scissors, white construction paper, stapler and/or masking tape

**Directions:**
1. On the background material, sketch an outline for the fort, then go over it with a felt marker.
2. Cut letters from white paper and darken the edges with black marker so they stand out.
3. Cut lots and lots of circles from white construction paper. (Suggested size: about 2 inches)

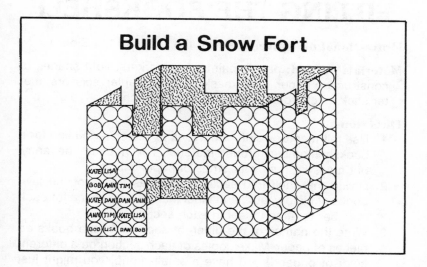

**Build a Snow Fort**

**Evaluation procedure:**
When the lesson is over, give white circles to the children who: have learned a different category of the books of the Bible such as the books of law, major and minor prophets, etc., the number of books in the entire Bible, know one or more verses about salvation, can say Psalm 100 or the Twenty-third Psalm, etc. These circles are placed on the fort and each child may write his or her name on their circles. The winner will have the most circles.

# FILLING THE BOOKSHELF

**Motivational objective:** Learning the books of the Bible

**Materials needed:** pencil, paints, felt markers, light shades of construction paper, glue, masking tape, stapler, scissors, meter stick, background material, a copy machine.

**Directions:**
1. Use felt marker, paint, or crayons to sketch an outline for a bookshelf on background material. This need not be fancy, but measure it so your strips of paper will fit.
2. Divide the shelf into sections such as books of the law, books of history, etc., and label them. Make space for each member to attach a set in each section.
3. Write the names of the different sections of the books on pieces of paper. Make copies of each section on a different color of paper. If you have a small group, you might just sketch them on colored paper and cut out.
4. Optional method: Draw the books on white paper and allow the students to color the sections with crayons, colored pencils, or chalk as the divisions are learned. Each child would have his or her own bookshelf on the board.

**Evaluation procedure:**
At the end of the class, each child who has recited the names of one section of the books of the Bible could attach them to the bookshelf in the proper place or color them.

# GARDEN OF KNOWLEDGE

**Motivational objective:** Learning the Scripture

**Materials needed:** large background material of light yellow, blue, or white paper or fabric, green and black felt markers, letter patterns, assorted colors of construction paper

### Directions:
1. Prepare the background. Then make vertical lines for the flowers with a green felt marker. Draw slender leaves, long and short, of various sizes.
2. Cut letters from bright-colored paper and use a felt marker to darken the edges.
3. Provide a box of various colors of construction paper for the students to use in making flowers.

### Evaluation procedure:
When all activities are completed, each child who has: found the specified verses first in the Bible drill, said the books of the Old and New Testaments, learned an assigned chapter or verse, or given the main idea of the lesson, may add a flower to the garden and write his or her name on it. Remember to recognize the winner in some way when the month is up.

# I WILL HIDE GOD'S WORD IN MY HEART

**Motivational objective:** Learning the Word of God

**Materials needed:** a large sheet of red construction paper or poster board, red paper for hearts, white background paper, felt markers or paints, thumbtacks or stapler

**Directions:**
1. Cover the board with white paper and make letters for the title.
2. Cut a very large heart from the red paper or poster board. Cut the bottom half of the heart again and staple or fasten this extra half onto the large heart to form a pocket.
3. Cut many small hearts from the red paper. If you have a small class, cut several for each member. A larger group could function better with one heart per member.

**Evaluation procedure:**
   A heart could be added to the pocket for memorizing the assigned Bible verse, learning the Bible story, memorizing the books of the Bible, etc. The larger group could add stars to their hearts. Be sure to put the children's names on their hearts.

# THE LIGHT OF THE WORLD

**Motivational objective:** Learning about the Bible

**Materials needed:** dark blue paper or fabric, light yellow construction paper, different colors of felt markers, masking tape or a stapler, letters for patterns

### Directions:
1. Cover the board with dark blue paper or fabric.
2. Lightly sketch in the word or words you wish to use. Then make a 2 inch circle for a pattern and use it to complete the outline of the one or more words in circles. Any Bible verse could be used.
3. Cut letters for the rest of the words from a light-colored paper and attach to the background.
4. From yellow paper, cut enough yellow circles to fill the circles in the words you have drawn on the board.

### Evaluation procedure:
After the lesson, those members who have learned the Bible verse, books of the Bible or those of the Old or New Testament, studied the lesson, named the twelve apostles, or learned a selected chapter, may add a light to the board. Be sure to write the student's name on his or her light. The winner is the one with the most lights.

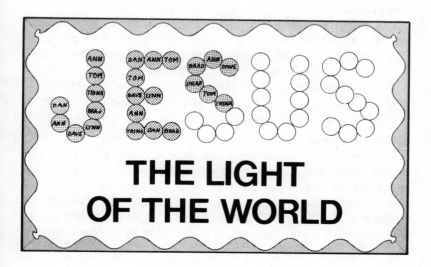

# MAKE YOUR BIRD FLY!

**Motivational objective:** Learning about the Bible

**Materials needed:** light blue background material, black felt marker, box or basket of crayons, colored pencils, a container of pieces of yellow, red, blue, and brown construction paper, scissors, glue, thumbtacks

**Directions:**
1. Cover the board and make letters for the title.
2. Draw horizontal lines across the board on the light blue background with the felt marker and number them. (Examples: 1, 2, 3, 4, 5, or 5, 10, 15, etc.)
3. Class members may make their own birds from the construction paper to fly from one line to the next. Names should be on the birds.

**Evaluation procedure:**
The birds are moved up each time a child learns an assigned Bible verse, can say the books of the Bible, knows how many books are in the Old or New Testament, learns the Twenty-third Psalm or any chapter selected that fits with your age group. As each child gets to the top, write his or her name in a specified place and return their birds to the first line to start over.

44

# PUT HONEY INTO THE HIVE

**Motivational objective:** Learning about the Bible

**Materials needed:** light background material, black, yellow, beige, or brown construction paper, felt markers, pencil, scissors, stapler or masking tape, thumbtacks, patterns for letters, crayons

## Directions:

1. Cut beehive and letters from brown or beige paper and outline them in black or brown felt marker.
2. Prepare background and arrange words and hive.
3. Cut bees from yellow paper and draw bands on them, or allow the children to color their own.
4. Draw vertical lines, beginning on the side away from the hive, and number them.

## Evaluation procedure:

When you have finished with the activities, each child who has learned the books of the Old or New Testament, the Twenty-third Psalm, Hundredth Psalm, names of the apostles, been first in Bible drill, etc., may move their bee toward the hive, one line for each activity.

# SCRIPTURE EGG HUNT

**Motivational objective:** Learning Bible verses

**Materials needed:** brightly-colored construction paper, felt markers, a pen or typewriter, a large piece of colored paper or poster board, glue, scissors, crayons or paints

**Directions:**
1. Cover the board with a light color. Cut letters from dark paper.
2. Cut eggs from brightly-colored construction paper. They should be large enough for a Bible verse on one side. Write the reference on the opposite side.
3. Make a large egg and decorate it. This large egg is where you will write the names of those who know their verses.
4. Hide the small eggs around the Sunday-school room for the children to find.
5. As a student finds an egg, he or she must say the verse if the reference side is showing. If the Scripture side is showing, then the reference must be given.

**Evaluation procedure:**
Each time a verse is memorized and the Scripture reference given, that child's name is written on the large egg. Don't forget the winner!

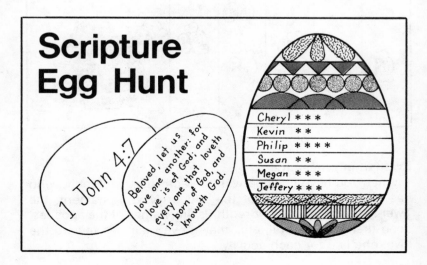

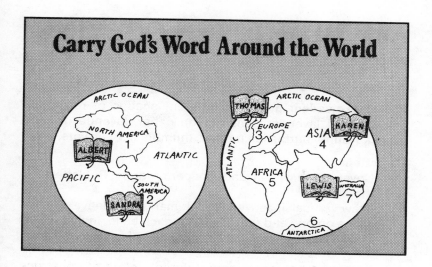

# CARRY GOD'S WORD

**Motivational objective:** Learning about missionaries

**Materials needed:** map of the world or large globe, black construction paper, white ink, scissors, pencils, strips of white paper, black or blue felt marker, background if you wish to use one with the map, thumbtacks

**Directions:**
1. Attach a large world map to the wall or use a background if you prefer.
2. For map markers, cut strips of white paper and write on them the names of the continents, numbers for each, and attach to the map or globe.
3. Cut small black Bibles from construction paper and, if you wish, write "BIBLE" on each in white. For easy identification, write each child's name on a Bible.

**Evaluation procedure:**
When you have finished with activities, each child who has brought an offering for the missionaries, learned names of missionaries, learned where one is going, brought a Bible to class, etc., may move once for each, around the map or globe. As each reaches the last continent, write his or her name on a list and keep track of points until the end of the designated period of time. Winners need recognition!

# MY HEART IS IN OBEYING

**Motivational objective:** Obeying God's commandments

**Materials needed:** a box of different shades of red, pink, white, and lavender construction paper, lavender for the background, purple felt marker, thumbtacks, scissors, glue

**Directions:**
1. Cover board with lavender paper or fabric. Cut letters for the title.
2. Draw vertical lines with the felt marker but leave enough space on one end for a heart for each child. In this space draw a heart for each child and write his or her name on it.
3. Prepare a box containing different colors of construction paper, glue, scissors, etc.
4. Let the children make hearts to move across the board.

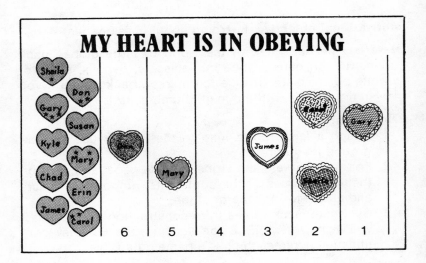

**Evaluation procedure:**

At the end of the lesson, each student gets a move for attendance, for learning the Bible verse, bringing a visitor, bringing an offering, or reporting on telling someone about Jesus. A child might get several moves at one time. As each reaches his or her heart, he or she would get a star or check on it. The winner is the one with the most stars or checks.